Shells

by Jennifer Boothroyd

first step nonfiction

Lerner Publications Company · Minneapolis

A **shell** is the hard outer
covering on an animal's body.

Many animals have shells.

Turtles have shells.

Snails have shells.

Some shells are smooth.

Some shells are bumpy.

Shells keep animals safe.

Clams shut themselves inside their shells.

Shells help animals hide.

This turtle is hard to see.

Shells come in different sizes.

When a tortoise grows, its shell grows too.

Lobsters **shed** old shells and grow new ones.

Hermit crabs do not grow
their own shells.

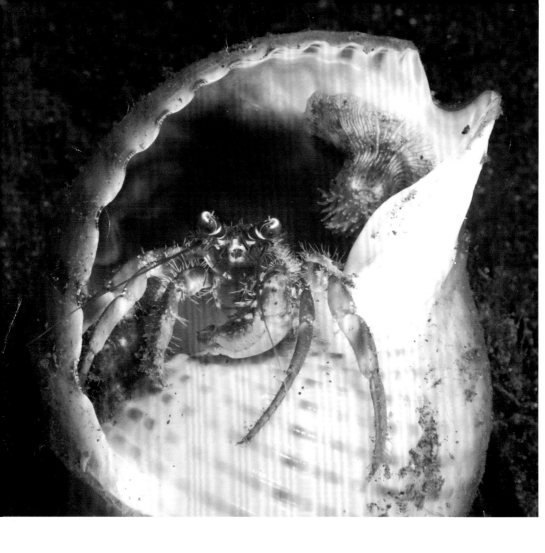

They live in the empty shells
of other animals.

Shells help animals in their surroundings.

Collecting Seashells

Many people collect seashells as a hobby.

Choose a beach that allows shell collecting. Bring a bag or a pail to hold your shells.

Walk along the beach. Make sure the shells you find are empty.

Wash and dry your shells at home. Rub them with oil to make them shine.

Learn what kinds of shells you found. The photos on page 19 can help.

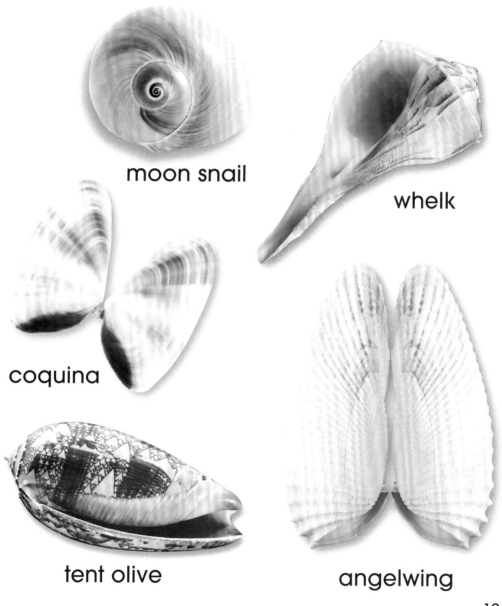

moon snail

whelk

coquina

tent olive

angelwing

19

Facts about Shells

 Seashells are made from layers of calcium carbonate. This material is also in bones.

 Turtle shells are made of keratin. Your fingernails are made of the same material.

 Most animals with shells do not have a backbone.

 Tortoises, turtles, and terrapins are **reptiles** with shells.

An **armadillo** is the only **mammal** with a shell.

 Giant clam shells can grow to 4 feet (1.2 meters) across.

 Shells were used as money thousands of years ago.

 A turtle never comes out of its shell. Its rib cage and backbone are part of the shell.

Glossary

 armadillo – a mammal with a hard but flexible shell

 mammal – a warm-blooded animal that drinks its mother's milk

 reptiles – animals with backbones that breathe air through their lungs

 shed – to lose or fall off

 shell – the hard outer covering on an animal's body

Index

The images in this book are used with the permission of: © Jurgen & Christine Sohns/Minden Pictures, pp. 2, 22 (top), (second from top); © EcoPrint/Shutterstock Images, p. 3; © Scott Leslie/Minden Pictures, pp. 4, 22 (third from top); © Georgette Douwma/naturepl.com, pp. 5, 22 (bottom); © Brandon Cole, pp. 6, 16, 17; © Interfoto/Zoology/Alamy, p. 7; © Serna/Dreamstime.com, p. 8; © Christopher Seufert Photography/Flickr/Getty Images, p. 9; © Jean E. Roche/naturepl.com, p. 10; © Hiroya Minakuchi/Minden Pictures, pp. 11; © Arco Images GmbH/Kiedrowski, R./Alamy, p. 12; © Jim Wileman/Alamy, p. 13; © Michele Hall/SeaPics.com, pp. 14, 22 (fourth from top); © Steven Kazlowski/SeaPics.com, p. 15; © Martin Shields/Alamy, p. 19 (top/left); © iStockphoto. com/yingyang0, p. 19 (top/right); © Zee/Alamy, p. 19 (middle left); © Victor R. Boswell Jr./National Geographic/Getty Images, p. 19 (bottom/left); © Perry Correll/Shutterstock Images, p. 19 (bottom/right).
Front Cover: © 2009 Gail Shotlander/Getty Images.

Main body text set in ITC Avant Garde Gothic 21/25. Typeface provided by Adobe Systems.

Lerner Publications Company
A division of Lerner Publishing Group, Inc.
241 First Avenue North
Minneapolis, MN 55401 U.S.A.

Website address: www.lernerbooks.com

Library of Congress Cataloging-in-Publication Data

Boothroyd, Jennifer, 1972–
    Shells / by Jennifer Boothroyd.
        p.   cm. — (First step nonfiction — Body coverings)
    Includes index.
    ISBN 978–0–7613–5788–9 (lib. bdg. : alk. paper)
    1. Shells—Juvenile literature. 2. Mollusks—Juvenile literature. 3. Turtles—Juvenile literature. 4. Decapoda (Crustacea)—Juvenile literature. I. Title.
    QL405.2.B66 2012
    594.147'7—dc22   2010050653

Manufactured in the United States of America
1 – PC – 7/15/11